THE ANIMAL FILES

WE NEED WOLVES

by Nancy Furstinger

FOCUS READERS

WWW.FOCUSREADERS.COM

Focus Readers is distributed by North Star Editions:
sales@northstareditions.com | 888-417-0195

Produced for Focus Readers by Red Line Editorial.

Content Consultant: Timothy R. Van Deelen, Professor of Forest and Wildlife Ecology, University of Wisconsin–Madison

Photographs ©: hkuchera/iStockphoto, cover, 1; Waddell Images/Shutterstock Images, 4–5; Red Line Editorial, 7, 15; Kenton D. Gomez/Shutterstock Images, 9; Harriet S/Shutterstock Images, 10–11; BlueBarronPhoto/Shutterstock Images, 13; Nagel Photography/Shutterstock Images, 16–17; flyinggrace/iStockphoto, 18–19; Lori Labrecque/Shutterstock Images, 21; MikeLane45/iStockphoto, 23; Andyworks/iStockphoto, 24–25; Carol M. Highsmith/Gates Frontiers Fund Colorado Collection/Carol M. Highsmith Archive/Library of Congress, 27; Thomas Sbampato/ImageBroker/Alamy, 29

Library of Congress Cataloging-in-Publication Data
Names: Furstinger, Nancy, author.
Title: We need wolves / by Nancy Furstinger.
Description: Lake Elmo, MN : Focus Readers, [2019] | Series: The animal files
  | Audience: Grade 4 to 6. | Includes index.
Identifiers: LCCN 2018037878 (print) | LCCN 2018038549 (ebook) | ISBN
  9781641854894 (PDF) | ISBN 9781641854313 (e-book) | ISBN 9781641853156
  (hardcover) | ISBN 9781641853736 (paperback)
Subjects: LCSH: Wolves--Ecology--Juvenile literature. |
  Wolves--Conservation--Juvenile literature.
Classification: LCC QL737.C22 (ebook) | LCC QL737.C22 F87 2019 (print) | DDC
  599.77--dc23
LC record available at https://lccn.loc.gov/2018037878

Printed in the United States of America
Mankato, MN
October, 2018

ABOUT THE AUTHOR

Nancy Furstinger is the author of nearly 100 books, including many on her favorite topic: animals! She has been a feature writer for a daily newspaper, a managing editor of trade and consumer magazines, and an editor at two children's book publishing houses. She shares her home with big dogs, house rabbits, and a chinchilla (all rescued).

TABLE OF CONTENTS

CHAPTER 1

HUNTING IN A PACK

A wolf howls from his perch on a rock. He's calling his pack. Earlier that day, the wolf saw a herd of elk. The elk were grazing in a field. Now, pack members gather around their leader. The wolves are ready to hunt.

One wolf stays to watch the **pups**. The rest of the pack sets off at a steady pace.

Wolves howl to communicate with one another.

After a few hours, the pack stops. The wolves sniff the air. The elk are nearby. The pack can sense other details, too. One elk in the herd is older and weaker than the rest. The wolves make this elk their target. They will work together to separate the elk from its herd. Then they will close in for the kill.

Gray wolves live in **ranges** throughout the Northern Hemisphere. They travel and hunt in grasslands, forests, and mountains. In North America, their range includes the Northern Rocky Mountains, the Pacific Northwest, and the Great Lakes region. It also stretches north into Canada and Alaska.

Gray wolves are the largest members of the **canine** family. From nose to tail, they can be up to 6 feet (1.8 m) long.

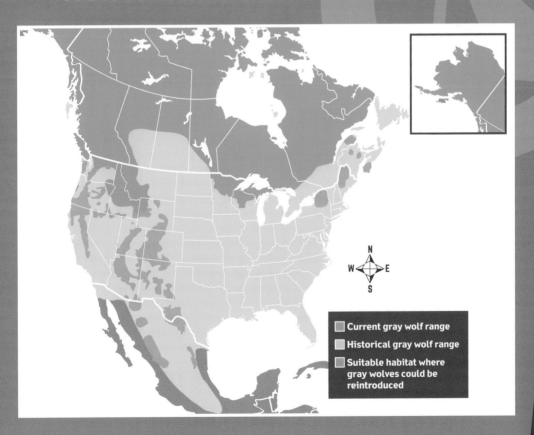

GRAY WOLVES IN NORTH AMERICA

N
W — E
S

Current gray wolf range

Historical gray wolf range

Suitable habitat where gray wolves could be reintroduced

They can weigh up to 135 pounds (61 kg). Not all gray wolves are gray. Their coats can also be white, black, or a mix of colors.

Wolves live and hunt in packs. One pack has approximately six wolves. The leader, or alpha, is the strongest and smartest wolf. The alpha male and female have litters together. Each litter has four to six pups. For the first two weeks, the pups cannot see or hear. But they already have a strong sense of smell. The members of the pack care for the pups. After a hunt, the wolves carry extra chunks of food in their stomachs. They bring the food back up to feed the pups.

Wolf pups learn to walk when they are two weeks old.

CHAPTER 2

A HEALTHY ECOSYSTEM

Wolves are a keystone **species**. This means they have a large effect on their **ecosystem**. Throughout the years, scientists have studied the effect of wolves in Yellowstone National Park. In the 1920s, the US government removed gray wolves from the park. Many people wanted to remove wolves from the West.

Today, the Greater Yellowstone Area is home to approximately 75 gray wolf packs.

They blamed wolves for killing **livestock**. But removing wolves from Yellowstone caused problems.

Gray wolves are predators. This means they hunt other animals for food. In Yellowstone, they hunted large **prey**, such as elk. They also hunted deer and moose. After a hunt, each wolf ate up to 20 pounds (9.1 kg) of meat. Wolves

IMPROVING THE SOIL

Wolves' hunting habits help keep soil healthy. Over time, bones and tissue from their prey decay. Scientists at a national park in Michigan studied how these materials affected the soil. The materials added nutrients that help plants grow.

Wild elk graze in Yellowstone National Park.

targeted old or sick animals. As a result, the rest of the prey population was healthy. By hunting, wolves also kept prey populations from growing too fast.

Without wolves, elk populations in Yellowstone soared. Elk overgrazed on trees, shrubs, and other plants. Their grazing caused fewer young trees to grow. This change affected many other species. Songbirds had fewer spots to nest.

Beavers had less food to eat. They also had less wood to build dams.

Coyotes no longer had to share their space with wolves. They became one of the park's top predators. Coyotes are smaller than wolves. Unlike wolves, they do not hunt larger prey. Instead, they eat small mammals. Some animals, such as foxes and eagles, relied on wolves' hunting habits. They would eat parts of elk after wolves had killed them. But without wolves, fewer elk were being hunted. Now, foxes and eagles had to compete with coyotes for food.

In 1995, the government started bringing wolves back to Yellowstone.

Afterward, the ecosystem began to heal. Once again, wolves preyed on elk. With fewer elk to graze, aspen and willow trees began to grow again. Then birds had more nesting areas. Beavers had more to eat and could build dams. The coyote population also fell to a healthy level.

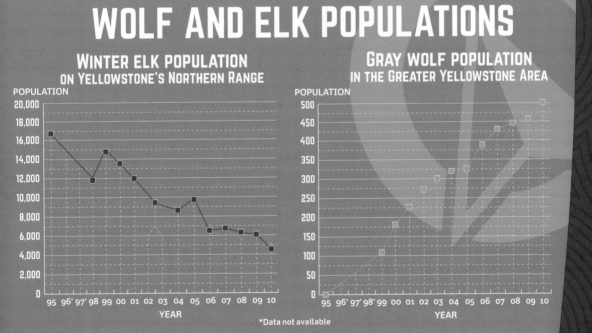

WOLF AND ELK POPULATIONS

WINTER ELK POPULATION
ON YELLOWSTONE'S NORTHERN RANGE

POPULATION

20,000
18,000
16,000
14,000
12,000
10,000
8,000
6,000
4,000
2,000
0

95 96ʻ97ʻ98ʻ99 00 01 02 03 04 05 06 07 08 09 10
YEAR
*Data not available

GRAY WOLF POPULATION
IN THE GREATER YELLOWSTONE AREA

POPULATION

500
450
400
350
300
250
200
150
100
50
0

95 96ʻ97ʻ98ʻ99 00 01 02 03 04 05 06 07 08 09 10
YEAR

WOLVES HELPING BEARS

The return of wolves to Yellowstone National Park helped another large predator. Without wolves, grizzly bears had been losing weight. Elk were grazing on shrubs that grew berries. This meant there were fewer berries for bears to eat.

Berries are an important part of a bear's diet. Scientists learned about bears' diets by studying the animals' waste. They found that the amount of berries in the waste doubles each August. Berries help bears gain weight before winter.

After wolves returned to the park, they preyed on elk. Wild berries could grow once again. With more berries to eat, grizzly bears began gaining weight.

A grizzly bear roams in Yellowstone National Park.

CHAPTER 3

THE BIGGEST THREAT

Throughout history, humans have struggled to share land with wolves. In the 1500s, settlers from Europe began arriving in North America. Many people in Europe were afraid of wolves. Settlers brought this fear to North America.

Some settlers thought gray wolves would attack humans without cause.

Some people hunt wolves to make furs.

But in reality, most wolves are afraid of humans. They try to stay away from people. Wolves, like other predators, can be dangerous. However, wolf attacks are very rare.

Settlers also thought gray wolves would compete with them for food. But wolves and humans tend to hunt different prey. Wolves tend to target large prey that are sick, old, or injured. Humans usually hunt young, healthy animals.

As North American towns grew, people began to farm and ranch. Ranchers raised livestock for food. To build their farms, settlers cleared land. They destroyed many **habitats** in the process. Afterward,

Gray wolves feed on a deer they hunted.

prey species dropped in number. Hungry wolves now needed other prey to eat. They started targeting livestock on farms and ranches.

Ranchers blamed wolves for losses to their livestock. But their livestock faced other, bigger threats. Disease and severe weather, such as droughts, killed more livestock than wolves.

In the 1800s and early 1900s, many people continued to view wolves as pests. They hired hunters to trap, shoot, and poison wolves. In 1906, the US Forest Service became involved. This agency hired trappers to rid cattle ranges of wolves. By the mid-1970s, gray wolves nearly vanished from the lower 48 states.

HONORING WOLVES

Many American Indian nations respect wolves. They admire wolves' hunting skills. They also value how packs live and hunt together. The Ojibwe consider wolves to be their brothers. And the Pawnee are known as the Wolf People. The nation uses the same hand signal to say "Pawnee" and "wolf."

Settlers used traps to catch and kill wolves.

Today, humans remain wolves' biggest threat. As the human population grows, cities and towns expand. People continue to settle on open land. As a result, wolves come into greater contact with humans. With greater contact, more killings of wolves take place.

CHAPTER 4

PROTECTING WOLVES

In 1973, the US Congress passed the Endangered Species Act (ESA). This new law gave protection to certain species. Endangered species are at risk of dying out. And threatened species are likely to become endangered. The ESA made it illegal to hunt animals in these categories.

A pack of wolves rests between hunts.

At first, gray wolves were listed as threatened. But in 1978, the US Fish and Wildlife Service changed the listing. Gray wolves in most of the lower 48 states were listed as endangered.

By 2011, gray wolf populations had increased in Idaho and Montana. For this reason, the animal was removed from the states' endangered species lists. Hunters could once again shoot gray wolves.

Gray wolf populations also rose in the Northern Rocky Mountains and Great Lakes region. Some **conservationists** wanted to remove wolves' protection status in more states. But many other conservationists were against this idea.

This wolf was rescued and cared for by the Wild Animal Sanctuary in Colorado.

Gray wolf populations were still low in places. Without protection, the species might not recover in Colorado and Utah.

Conservationists work to protect gray wolves. They also try to solve problems that wolves cause. For example, some ranchers use dogs to protect livestock.

They raise dogs alongside their sheep. They train the dogs to stand between sheep and predators. Other ranchers use electric fences.

Tourists can also help gray wolves. People come from around the world to

WOLF AWARENESS WEEK

Defenders of Wildlife is a group that works to protect wolves. Every October, the group celebrates Wolf Awareness Week. During this week, the group offers ideas about how people can support wolves. It educates people about wolves' importance to ecosystems. Defenders of Wildlife hopes to expand wolf ranges. The group also offers solutions to ranchers' problems with wolves. Sometimes, the group pays ranchers for the livestock wolves kill.

An alpha wolf (right) wears a tracking collar put on by scientists.

visit Yellowstone National Park. They can see the park's wolf packs. These wolves were all born in the park.

Yellowstone uses tourists' money to pay researchers. Researchers put tracking collars on some of the wolves. They use these collars to study the wolves' activity. The more researchers learn, the more they can do to protect the species.

FOCUS ON
WOLVES

Write your answers on a separate piece of paper.

1. Write a paragraph summarizing the main ideas of Chapter 3.

2. Do you think gray wolves should be protected in all of the lower 48 states? Why or why not?

3. Which animals became the top predators in Yellowstone when wolves were removed?

> **A.** foxes
>
> **B.** elk
>
> **C.** coyotes

4. What might happen today if wolves were removed from Yellowstone?

> **A.** More young trees would grow.
>
> **B.** The elk population would increase.
>
> **C.** More park rangers would be hired.

Answer key on page 32.

GLOSSARY

canine
Relating to or having the traits of a dog.

conservationists
People who protect plants and animals.

ecosystem
The collection of living things in a natural area.

habitats
The type of places where plants or animals normally grow or live.

livestock
Animals that farmers raise for the purpose of making money.

prey
Animals that are hunted and eaten by a different animal.

pups
Babies or young wolves.

ranges
The areas where a certain kind of animal naturally lives.

species
A group of animals or plants that are similar.

tourists
People who visit an area for recreation.

TO LEARN MORE

BOOKS

Dutcher, Jim, and Jamie Dutcher. *Living with Wolves!: True Stories of Adventures with Animals.* Washington, DC: National Geographic, 2016.

Smith, Paula. *Bringing Back the Gray Wolf.* New York: Crabtree Publishing, 2018.

Wallace, Audra. *Yellowstone National Park.* New York: Children's Press, 2018.

NOTE TO EDUCATORS

Visit **www.focusreaders.com** to find lesson plans, activities, links, and other resources related to this title.

INDEX

Answer Key: 1. Answers will vary; **2.** Answers will vary; **3.** C; **4.** B